Praise for Other Books by Fred Fuld III

Stock Market Trivia

"It is refreshingly different and very fun. It is very much out of the ordinary and unusual." ~ **Ken Fisher, Founder & Chairman of Fisher Investments, former** *Forbes* **columnist, billionaire, and author**

"Great fun" ~ **Steve Forbes, publisher** *Forbes Magazine*

"Interesting book" ~ **Warren Buffett, billionaire investor**

"Anything that helps educate the public on the financial services industry is laudable. I'll share it with my office staff." ~ **T. Boone Pickens, billionaire, chairman of the hedge fund BP Capital Management**

"The history of the stock market and its primary financial hub, on Wall Street, is quite fascinating, and it's all right here in this engaging trivia guide. Anyone fascinated with history and another compelling slice of American pop culture will certainly enjoy perusing these pages!" ~ **Larry Underwood, author** *Life Under the Corporate Microscope*

"It is a fun book that sheds some light on what many may consider a boring world of stocks and bonds. It's a quick read and will come in handy at the office to lighten and enlighten those who may be lacking in knowledge of stock terms and history. And, of course, it will make a good reference for playing finance related trivia matches." ~ **pfaulhaber, blogcritics.org**

"A fun, fact-filled book for those working with investments, be it on a personal or a professional level." ~ **SeattlePI.com**

"Have you ever wondered where the stock market terms bull and bear came from? How about where and when the first stockbroker took up the trade? Do you know what PINES, QUIBS and PDs are? A new book by Fred Fuld III." ~ **PulpLit Magazine**

"A fun, enjoyable read! This book provides a nice break from all the investment analysis and methodologies you find in other stock market books. A pleasant offering of fun facts and trivia that keep the pages turning. Well done." ~ **Dan K., Hedge Fund Manager**

"As someone who has always found money and investments to be painfully boring, I'm glad someone has introduced a lighter tone to such dry subjects. Fuld unearths such gems as the smallest stock exchange in the world, the Wall Street billionaire who starred in a TV soap opera, the stock that traded for more than $1 million a share, the firm that paid more than $8.5 million for a domain name, and the stock that owned a rock with George Washington's graffiti on it. " ~ **Tom Elliott, The Magazine of American Mensa**

Let Me Entertain You with Antique Stock Certificates

"I am a history buff, as well as a long time certificate collector. I enjoyed Fred's research and lively writing style, and am very pleased to see another highly readable book in the scripophily collecting area."
~ **John E. Herzog, former Chairman R. M. Smythe & Co., Inc., founder of Museum of American Finance, former Chairman & CEO of Herzog Heine Geduld, Inc.**

Real Estate Trivia 2019

The Fun Side of Homes, Houses, Land, and Property

Fred Fuld III

No part of this book may be reproduced, stored in a retrieval system, or transmitted by any means in whole or in part without the express written permission of the author. However, the ShareAlike terms of Creative Commons for the pictures may be followed.

All trademarks, registered trademarks, service marks, and registered service marks are owned by their respective trademark, registered trademark, service mark, and registered service mark owners. The author and publisher do not claim ownership of these trademarks, servicemarks, brands, or logos. Images of documents, currency, and certificates are shown for educational purposes based on the Fair Use section of the Copyright Act of 1976, 17 U.S.C. § 107.

This publication is sold with the understanding that the author and publisher are not engaged in providing real estate advice, investment advice, tax advice or legal advice. The author and publisher specifically disclaim any liability that is incurred from the use of the content of this book. Information provided in the book is believed to be accurate but is not guaranteed.

Copyright © 2018 Fred Fuld III

All rights reserved.

ISBN-13: 978-1729846698
ISBN-10: 1729846696

CONTENTS

	Introduction	v
Chapter 1	Tax Sale of 1 Square Inch of Land	9
Chapter 2	Smallest Parcel of Land in New York City	11
Chapter 3	Big Houses - Palaces	13
Chapter 4	Big Houses - Castles	15
Chapter 5	Biggest Mansion in the World-	17
Chapter 6	Biggest Mansion in the U.S.	19
Chapter 7	Smallest Town Sold – Population 1	21
Chapter 8	Red Front Doors	23
Chapter 9	Lighthouses	25
Chapter 10	Winchester Mystery House	27
Chapter 11	Most Expensive House in the U.S.	31
Chapter 12	Famous Real Estate Quotations	33
Chapter 13	Monopoly	39
Chapter 14	Warren Buffett's Real Estate	43
Chapter 15	3D Printed Houses	45
Chapter 16	Tiniest House	47
Chapter 17	The Narrowest House	49
Chapter 18	The White House	51
Chapter 19	Ice Hotels	55
Chapter 20	First Motel	57
Chapter 21	First Hotel	59
Chapter 22	Weird Town Names	61
Chapter 23	The Woman Who Said No to Penthouse and Trump	65
Chapter 24	Trading a Paperclip for a House	67
Chapter 25	Islands	69
Chapter 26	Miscellaneous Trivia	73
	Sources	77
	Picture Credits	89
	About the Author	93

Fred Fuld III

INTRODUCTION

    Five years ago, I wrote *Stock Market Trivia* which became one of the top selling investment and trivia books at that time, with rave reviews from investors, journalists, and billionaires. I recently wrote a new trivia book called *Investment Trivia 2019,* about investments in general, not just stocks, which includes updated material and lots of new trivia.

    However, even though real estate is also an investment, many consider it to be in a category by itself. So I decided to create a trivia book about houses and land.

    Who says that real estate is boring? If you think so, your opinion will change after reading this book.

Real Estate Trivia 2019

Chapter 1

Tax Sale of 1 Square Inch of Land

Many people go to tax sales to try to get a bargain on a house, land, and other types of property. Some of the strangest properties crop up at these auctions, usually held by counties for non-payment of back property taxes.

There have been properties a foot wide and 50 feet long (maybe perfect for a billboard?), totally landlocked properties with no street access, underwater properties, islands, and many other non-typical lots.

Although there have been a few fundraising or money-raising schemes whereby someone or some organization sells off one square inch parcels of their property, there is possibly only one government sponsored sale of a one inch parcel.

In 2005, Owen County in Indiana had an interesting parcel up for sale at auction. It was a one inch piece of land located in a wealthy area of the county west of Bloomington, with a minimum bid of $1,500.

The property didn't sell and was looking to donate it to Owen County Preservations. The county believes that the tiny lot was originally created from a larger lot owner who may have given one square inch to a friend or relative so that they could have access to a nearby lake.

This would probably make it the smallest property sale by a government, the most expensive piece of land based on an acreage price, and possibly the smallest land donation.

Chapter 2

Smallest Parcel of Land in New York City
27.5 inches at its Longest Side

There is a very tiny parcel of land in New York City in the shape of a triangle, measuring 27.5 inches (70 cm) on two of the sides and 25.5 inches (65 cm) on the third side.

This tiny parcel located at the corner of Seventh Avenue and Christopher Street in the West Village neighborhood is called the Hess Triangle.

Image via Wikimedia Commons - Bogframe

It came about because, David Hess, the original owner of the Voorhis apartment building, which included the triangle as part of the apartment parcel, did not want to give up his building for redevelopment. The city took over the building by eminent domain but accidentally left out the tiny corner of the property, which was discovered by Hess's family in the early 1900's.

The city asked the family to give the property to them, but the family refused and installed a plaque, similar to the Hollywood Walk of Fame Stars, except this one was in the shape of a triangle, matching the boundaries of the land. It was placed on July 27, 1922.

The plaque reads:

> PROPERTY OF THE
> HESS ESTATE
> WHICH HAS NEVER
> BEEN DEDICATED
> FOR PUBLIC
> PURPOSES

The property was eventually sold by the family to the Village Cigars store, which is currently on the main corner lot, in 1938. The price was $1,000.

The plaque is still there at the time of this writing, cracked and spotted with gum.

Chapter 3

Big Houses - Palaces

Who wouldn't want to live in a big mansion or a giant castle? In order to determine what the biggest house is, we have to look at what is considered to be a house.

A palace is generally considered to be the residence of the head of a country's government, or it could also be the home of a bishop or archbishop.

If we include palaces, then the largest is the Palace of the Parliament in Romania, with floor space totaling 3,930,000 square feet (365,000 square meters).

Palace of the Parliament

It was created for the Communist dictator Nicolae Ceaușescu, and completed in 1987 after 13 years of construction. Ceaușescu didn't need it any more by December of 1989 as he was overthrown during the Romnian Revolution. It now houses the Romanian parliament along with several museums.

The building has 1,100 rooms and is now considered to be the second largest administration building in the world. (The Pentagon is first.)

Other record-setting palaces include Hofburg Palace in Austria at 2,583,339 square feet, which sets the record for the largest palace where a head of state currently lives. It is the official residence of Alexander Van der Bellen, the President of Austria.

The largest functioning royal palace in the world is Istana Nurul Iman in Brunei. It measures out at 2,152,782 square feet.

The world's largest palace complex is the Forbidden City in Beijing, China, with a total floor area of 1,614,587 square feet, but a total enclosed area of 178 acres.

Chapter 4

Big Houses - Castles

The largest castle in the world is Malbork Castle, in Malbork, Poland. It was built in 1274 by the Teutonic Knights. It has total floor space of 1,539,239 square feet. By the way, Windsor Castle is only 590,239 square feet.

Malbork Castle

Chapter 5

Biggest Mansion in the World

The largest private residence in the world is called Antilia, located on Altamount Road, Cumballa Hill in Mumbai, India. This 27 story house cost approximately $2 billion to build, making also the most expensive private residential home. The chairman of Reliance Industries, Mukesh Ambani, is the owner of the property.

©A.Savin, Wikimedia Commons

This house has a bunch of trivia all its own. Here is a list of interesting facts about the property.

It has floor space of 400,000 square feet
It is the tallest home in the world
The house has a staff of 600
It has three helicopter pads
It is built on land which originally housed an orphanage
The house is named after Antilas, the mythic island
It has ten elevators
It has extra high ceilings
It is earthquake proof up to 8 on the Richter Scale
It was built by an Australian construction company
It has a 160 car capacity in its underground parking lot

Chapter 6

Biggest Mansion in the U.S.

In the United States, the largest privately owned mansion is the Biltmore Estate, located in Asheville, North Carolina. George Washington Vanderbilt II had the home built beginning in the year 1889 and was completed in 1895, using over 1,000 workers.

The house has 178,926 square feet (16,622.8 square meters) of floor space. This 35 bedroom, 43 bathroom home has 65 fireplaces and three kitchens.

Guests who have stayed there include Presidents William McKinley, Theodore Roosevelt, Woodrow Wilson, Jimmy Carter, Ronald Reagan, and Barack Obama.

Biltmore Estate - 24dupontchevy -via Wikipedia

Chapter 7

Smallest Town Sold – Population 1

How would you like to own your own town with a gas station, store, and home on 9.9 acres? This town, located in Albany County, Wyoming, was originally called Buford and is now named PhinDeli Town Buford, was put up for auction in 2013.

The town, named after Major General John Buford, was founded in 1866 while the Transcontinental Railroad was being built.

The auction had a minimum bid of $100,000 and it sold for $900,000.

At the time of the sale, the population of the town was one, down from 2,000 at its height in the 1800s.

Flickr - Mark Brennan

Chapter 8

Red Front Doors

If you have ever notices that some houses have front doors that are painted in red, especially in Scotland, you might have wondered what the meaning is.

Here is a list of the red door meaning from around the world, with different cultures, and history.

1. In ancient times, the blood of a lamb was smeared on front doors in order to provide protection from the Angel of Death.
2. During the early days of the Catholic Church, the doors of the churches were painted red which represented the blood of Christ, and often meant evil protection.
3. In Scotland, when the owners of a home paid off their mortgage, they would paint their front door red to show that they now own their homes free and clear.
4. In Feng Shui, it means that the home has welcoming energy or that the red color will provide positive energy.
5. In China, many homeowners paint or re-paint their front doors red on Chinese New Year for luck.
6. During the early days of the United States, the red door signified that weary travelers were welcome to stop and rest.
7. The Underground Railroad used it as a sign that the house was a safe place for slaves in the pre-Civil War era.

Chapter 9

Lighthouses

If you like isolation, then maybe living in a lighthouse is for you. These tall structures have provided navigational assistance for ships for thousands of years.

The first lighthouse is believed to be the Lighthouse of Alexandria, completed around 246 BC. It was approximately 330 feet (100 meters) tall and one of the Seven Ancient Wonders of the World.

Living in Your Own Lighthouse

Back in 2007, if your were looking for that special vacation home or corporate retreat, away from everything, you could have bought yourself a lighthouse. It would be like having your own island with a house on it. The U. S. Government sold off dozens of these lighthouses, with prices starting at $10,000.

In 2010, Plum Island, located at the eastern end of Long Island, was considered to be put up for sale by the General Services Administration. Unfortunately for potential island and lighthouse buyers, the plan to sell was put on hold. Currently, the island is used for an animal disease laboratory. The island has 840 acres with a lighthouse and a beach.

Chapter 10

Winchester Mystery House

If you are ever in California, and you have never been to it, you need to check out the Winchester Mystery House, strangely located almost in the heart of Silicon Valley.

This was formerly the personal home of Sarah Lockwood Pardee Winchester, wife of William Wirt Winchester, co-founder of the Winchester Repeating Arms Company. After her husband died and she inherited over $20 million plus almost half of the Winchester company, she moved from New Haven, Connecticut to California and had construction begun on her house in 1884. The house has many quirks, including a skylight in the floor, windows where you can see into other rooms, Doors that open up to walls, stairs that led nowhere, and ghosts.

Winchester Mystery House - National Park Service

Here is some trivia on this famous house.

1. Many reports saw that a fortune teller told Sarah Winchester that she needed to move west and build a home, not just for herself, but for the ghosts of people who died from Winchester rifles.
2. Sarah Winchester could afford to build her mansion because she received **$1,000 per day** (about $25,700 in today's dollars) from her Winchester inheritance.
3. The house was reportedly being constructed 24 hours a day and never ceased until Sarah Winchester's death.
4. The house was originally seven stories, but after the 1906 Earthquake, it was rebuilt to four stories.
5. There are 161 rooms altogether.
6. The house had 40 bedrooms.
7. Fires can be built in the house's 47 fireplaces.
8. The various floors can be accessed with three different elevators.
9. The house was painted with over 20,000 gallons of paint.
10. Windows in the house contain more than 10,000 panes of glass.
11. The house had only one working toilet, with the rest of the bathrooms for the ghosts.
12. Sarah Winchester designed a stained glass window which had the number 13 displayed over and over again, but the window was never installed, currently sitting in a storage room.

13. Speaking of the number 13, the number is repeated in various ways throughout the house.
14. The house has been able to avoid total destruction from all major California earthquakes due to its construction on a floating foundation.
15. The house was not mentioned in Sarah Winchester's will.
16. After her death in 1922, the mansion was sold for $135,000.
17. The first tours of the home were given in February of 1923.
18. A previously unknown room was discovered in the house in 2016.

Chapter 11

Most Expensive House for Sale in the U.S.

The One

By the time you read this, the most expensive house for sale in the United States may have changed, as the current expensive house may be sold or another more expensive mansion may come on the market.

Currently, at the time this was written, the most expensive house has a unique name of The One. It is located in the tony Bel Air area of Los Angeles and is reasonably priced at $500,000,000. The developer was real estate tycoon Niles Niami and the architect was Paul McClean.

Here are some details about it.
1. The house has a 360 degree view.
2. There are 20 bedrooms.
3. There are 27 bathrooms.
4. It contains a 40 seat movie theater.
5. A four-lane bowing alley is also included.
6. It even has a night club.
7. There are four swimming pools.
8. A moat encircles the property.
9. Some of the walls are made with jellyfish tanks.
10. At a 100,000 square feet, it is almost twice the size of the White House.
11. It includes a 30 car garage.
12. Famous neighbors include Elon Musk and Jennifer Anniston.

* * *

Chartwell

In second place is an estate called Chartwell, also located in Bel Air. This 11 bedroom, 18 bathroom home is up for sale at $245 million, marked down from $350 million.

Here is some information about this mansion.
1. The house was owned by the late TV executive Jerry Perenchio
2. There is 25,000 square feet of floor space.
3. It was built in the early 1930s.
4. This is the house that appeared in *The Beverly Hillbillies* TV show
5. The car gallery can accommodate 40 vehicles.
6. It includes a five bedroom guest house.
7. The wince cellar can accommodate 12,000 wine bottles.

Beverly Hillbillies Mansion – Photo by Alan Light

Chapter 12

Famous Real Estate Quotations

"I'm a businesswoman. You know, I have other investments too, real estate. A long time ago, I would buy a house and flip it. But now everybody does that, so I don't do that anymore because there's no houses out there to buy."
~ Vanna White

"To my real estate agent, Chernobyl is a fixer-upper."
~ Yakov Smirnoff

"We never had it as rough as the kids have it today. Look at the price of a gallon of gas or a piece of real estate or a college education."
~ Suze Orman

"Real estate is the key cost of physical retailers. That's why there's the old saw: location, location, location."
~ Jeff Bezos

"What we call real estate - the solid ground to build a house on - is the broad foundation on which nearly all the guilt of this world rests."
~ Nathaniel Hawthorne

"I weirdly love interior design and real estate and all of that. I really do. I get chills from it."
~ Kendall Jenner

"South Sydney is a very complicated and wonderful place. You have some of the most expensive bits of real estate in the country and a large percentage of government housing."
~ Russell Crowe

"Commercial real estate is really a black box: its super opaque, and it's hard to get the information."
~ Jason Calacanis

"I don't think acting is addictive. If I stopped acting tomorrow, I really wouldn't care. If you told me that I would have to sell real estate in New York City to look after my family, that would be fine with me."
~ Alec Baldwin

"The wise young man or wage earner of today invests his money in real estate."
~ Andrew Carnegie

"In so far as Government lands can be disposed of, I am in favor of cutting up the wild lands into parcels, so that every poor man may have a home."
~ Abraham Lincoln

"Real estate is the best investment for small savings. More money is made from the rise in real estate values than from all other causes combined."
~ William Jennings Bryan

"Real estate cannot be lost or stolen nor can it be carried away. Purchased with common sense, paid for in full, and managed with reasonable care it is about the safest investment in the world."
~ Franklin D Roosevelt

"No investment on earth is so safe, so sure, so certain to enrich its owner as undeveloped realty. I always advise my friends to place their savings in realty near some growing city."
~ Grover Cleveland

"Current real estate prices aren't high because they have been driven up by irresponsible speculation. As was often the case in the past. Prices have risen because a constantly increasing population with money to invest has been created - and continues to be created."
~ J.Paul Getty

"The Major fortunes in America have been made in land."
~ John D. Rockefeller

"Don't wait to buy real estate. Buy real estate and wait."
~ Will Rogers

"Real estate investing, even on a very small scale, remains a tried and true means of building an individual's cash flow and wealth."
~ Robert Kiyosaki

"Real estate is my life. It is my day job, if you will. But it consumes my nights and weekends, too."
~ Ivanka Trump

"First and foremost, I'm a real estate person. And that's what I love the most."
~ Donald Trump

"I view real estate as the most intriguing opportunity that I've seen in my business lifetime."
~ Richard Rainwater

"I had probably seven agents by the time I became a legitimate real estate broker."
~ Barbara Corcoran

"I own a mortgage company and a real estate company funded by the music. Florida is a kinda gold mine."
~ Vanilla Ice

"I've always wanted to be the biggest real estate man to come down the pike."
~ Leona Helmsley

"Half of this business is politics. As real estate developers, it's our job to go in there and get beat up."
~ Ross Perot, Jr.

"Buy land. They ain't making any more of the stuff."
~Will Rogers

"The land belongs to those who work it with their hands."
~ Emiliano Zapata

"Men did not make the earth... It is the value of the improvements only, and not the earth itself, that is individual property."
~ Thomas Paine

"The first man who, having fenced off a plot of land, thought of saying, 'This is mine' and found people simple enough to believe him was the real founder of civil society."
~ Jean-Jacques Rousseau

"Property is surely a right of mankind as really as liberty."
~ John Adams

"There is no place like home."
~ Judy Garland

Chapter 13

Monopoly

The most popular real estate board game ever created is Monopoly®. The game where you try to buy as much property as possible, bring in as much rent as possible, and drive your opponents into bankruptcy. It is licensed in more than 103 different countries.

Here are some trivia items about the game.

1. It was originally based on a game called The Landlord's Game in 1903.
2. On February 6, 1935, Parker Brothers began selling the game.
3. During World War II, the British Secret Service had a special version of the game made for British soldiers held in Nazi prisoner of war camps. The game contained hidden escape items including cash and maps.
4. Parker Brothers had only two versions of the game, regular and deluxe.
5. Hasbro bought out Parker Brothers in 1991, along with the rights to Monopoly.
6. There are now over 100 licensee versions of the game.
7. The properties are named after locations in or near Atlantic City, New Jersey.
8. In 1990, there was a Monopoly TV game show.
9. Hasbro allowed Internet bidding to determine what landmarks should appear on the *Monopoly Here and Now* edition of the game.

10. Pre-September 2008 versions of the game had $15,140 in Monopoly money, and the current version has $20,580.
11. Original tokens that are still in use are the Battleship, Racecar, and the Top Hat.
12. The Scottie Dog has been in use since 1942 and is still in use.
13. In 2017, Hasbro released a 64-token limited edition set called Monopoly Signature Token Collection which included all of the tokens that were not chosen that year through the online vote.
14. The longest game of Monopoly ever played lasted 1,680 hours.
15. There are *Monopoly*-themed slot machines and lotteries.
16. The most expensive Monopoly set was valued at $2,000,000. It was made with rubies and sapphires and utilized 23 carat gold. It is currently in the Smithsonian Institution.
17. The most expensive set available to the public was called One-Of-A-Kind Monopoly and sold by FAO Schwartz for $100,000 in the year 2000. It had 18 carat gold hotels, houses, and tokens. It also was made with rubies, sapphires, and emeralds. To top it off, it contained real U.S. currency!

Real Estate Trivia 2019

Chapter 14

Warren Buffett's Real Estate

Everyone is familiar with Warren Buffett, one of the wealthiest people in the world. Most people are aware of Buffett's success with stocks, but he also has a connection to real estate.

* * *

Warren Buffett still lives in the same house he bought in 1958 for $31,500, in Omaha, Nebraska.

This 5 bedroom and 2.5 bathroom two-story home has 6,570 square feet.

* * *

Warren Buffett has owned a home in Laguna Beach, California since 1971 and sold it in October of 2018. He paid $150,000 for the home, but had a tough time selling it, as he listed it for $11 million in 2017, but had to drop the price by over $3 million in August of 2018, finally selling it for $7.47 million in October of 2018.

The 3,588-square-foot house is located about a block from the ocean. The house has six bedrooms, seven bathrooms, and is located in the Emerald Bay gated community.

* * *

Warren Buffett's Berkshire Hathaway owns only one real estate investment trust, Store Capital. The company specializes in net lease retail and service based commercial properties.

* * *

Warren Buffett's Berkshire Hathaway owns HomeServices of America Inc., the second largest real estate brokerage firm in the United States.

The company generates over $2 billion in revenues, has more than $7 billion in total assets, and has 1,600 employees.

* * *

"If you know you're going to live in a given area, or think it's very likely, for a considerable period of time and you've got a family, the home is terrific." ~ Warren Buffett

Warren Buffett at the White House

Chapter 15

3D Printed Houses

Can you imagine having a house printed for you? It's not only possible, houses have been created through 3D printing for some time.

The advantages of 3D printed houses are lower costs, faster building, less waste, and more accurate construction.

The first residential printed building was constructed in Yaroslavl, Russia with an area of 3,213 square feet. The walls were 3D printed in a shop and assembled at the site. The building was completed in 2017.

AMT-SPETSAVIA Group - 1st 3D printed building in Europe

* * *

COBOD International has just completed a small office hotel building using the building-on-demand technique with a 3D printed wall and foundation structure, making it the first building of its kind in Europe.

The flexibility of its construction is shown by its use of curved walls and a rippling effect for the surfaces.

Office Hotel - 3DPrinthuset (Denmark)

Chapter 16

Tiniest House

How would you like to live in a house where the total square footage is less than 400 square feet? That's just 20 feet by 20 feet. If you wouldn't mind that type of living environment, then a tiny house might be right for you, as anything less than 400 feet is considered tiny.

If you think 400 square feet is small, how would you like to live in a house that is only twenty-five square feet in size! That's right, 3.5 feet wide by 7.2 feet long, with a ceiling height of slightly over 3 feet.

It is so small, it can even fit in the back of a truck or a van.

If it sounds like it isn't much different than a coffin, you would be wrong, as the house has lots of amenities, including a sink, a stovetop, and a toilet. There is even a shower that will wash you with a quart of water.

The home was designed by Jeff Smith of Boston, Massachusetts, an artist, builder, and filmmaker. He appeared on ABC's "To Tell the Truth" TV show in 2017. He actually created a documentary about a man who lived in the house for a while.

If you are interested, the house is available for rent on Airbnb.

Chapter 17

The Narrowest House

The narrowest house in the world is the Keret House in Warsaw, Poland. The house is 3 feet wide at its narrowest (92 centimeters) at its narrowest and slightly less than five feet (152 centimeters) at its widest.

The house, which has one, bedroom, one bathroom, one kitchen, and one living room, was built between a pre-World War II house and an apartment building.

The house was named after the first tenant of the house, Etgar Keret, an Israeli filmmaker and writer.

The home was designed by the architect Jakub Szczęsny, but is considered an art installation because it doesn't meet the building codes of Poland, in spite of the fact that someone is living there.

To get from one level to the next, you use a ladder, and the retractable stairs at the entrance turn into a living room when closed. The house has its own water and sewerage system.

If you happen to be in Warsaw and want to check it out, it is located between 22 Chłodna Street and 74 Żelazna Street.

Keret House in Warsaw - Panek - Own Work

Chapter 18

The White House

The White House needs no introduction, as it is the official residence and office of the President of the United States. Here is some trivia about this home.

1. The street address of the White House is 1600 Pennsylvania Avenue NW in Washington, D.C.

2. There was a competition to determine the design of the White House with nine submissions, including one by Thomas Jefferson who submitted it anonymously.

3. The architect of the White House, James Hoban, was from Ireland.

4. The only president who has never lived in the White House was George Washington.

5. The Executive Residence has six stories, including two basements.

6. The original names of the White House were the "President's Palace", "Presidential Mansion", or "President's House".

7. President Theodore Roosevelt changed the name to "White House–Washington" in 1901.

8. Franklin D. Roosevelt changed the name to "The White House" during his administration.

9. During John Adams' second day in office, he wrote to his wife "May none but honest and wise men ever rule under this roof."

10. During the Carter administration, the first computers and laser printer were installed.

11. The White House was one of the first wheelchair-accessible government buildings in Washington, under the administration of Franklin D. Roosevelt.

12. There is 55,000 square feet of floor space.

13. It has 35 bathrooms.

14. It has three elevators.

15. It has 28 fireplaces.

16. There is a swimming pool, putting green, tennis court, movie theater, and bowling alley.

17. It sits on 18 acres.

18. The north front of the White House appears on the back of the U.S. $20 bill.

19. Benjamin Harrison had the first electric lights installed in the White House, but he was afraid of electricity.

20. In 1877, President Rutherford B. Hayes banned liquor at the White House.

Chapter 19

Ice Hotels

Ice Hotels, you can guess, are hotels made out of ice. They are rebuilt every year. There are two major ice hotels, The Ice Hotel in Quebec and Icehotel in Sweden.

The Ice Hotel in Quebec

The Ice Hotel, near Quebec City, in Quebec, Canada, is the first ice hotel in North America.
It first opened in 2001 with 11 double beds. It currently has 51 double beds, all made out of ice. The walls are as much as four feet thick. The heated bathrooms are in a separate structure.
It takes 500 tons of ice and 50,000 tons of snow to build, with 50 workers.

* * *

Icehotel in Jukkasjärvi

The Icehotel in Jukkasjärvi, Sweden, is the first ice hotel in the world.
It first opened in 1990, with all the bods and chairs made from ice and snow. The hotel has a bar where the glasses are made out of ice.
There are approximately 100 rooms, none of which have bathrooms. The bathrooms are in a structure by the hotel.
In addition to being the first, it is also the largest ice hotel in the world at 64,600 square feet.
You can see the aurora borealis from the hotel.

Chapter 20

First Motel

The first motel in the world was the Milestone Mo-Tel, now known as The Motel Inn. It was built in San Luis Obispo, California on December 12, 1925, at a cost of $80,000.

The architecture was based on Spanish missions.

The motel had a room rate of $1.25 per night.

Unfortunately, the motel was closed in 1991, but a couple buildings remain. If you happen to be in San Luis Obispo and you want to see it, it is located at 2223 Monterey Street.

First Motel

Chapter 21

First Hotel

The country of Japan seems to have corners the market on oldest hotels as the three oldest are located there. The first hotel in the world is Koshu Nishiyama Hot Spring - Keiunkan, also known as Nishiyama Onsen Keiunkan, which has been operating for more than 1,300 years in Hayakawa, in the Yamanashi Prefecture.

It is a hot spring hotel which means that it gets its water from volcanic springs, in this case, the Hakuho Springs. The hotel offers six kinds of baths, all with spring water.

The hotel was founded in 705 AD and has been operated by the same family since that time.

In case you are interested in visiting it, the hotel currently has 35 rooms available, and also offers both hot and cold dishes prepared by a chef who received an award from the Four Seasons.

The second oldest hotel is Koman and the third oldest hotel is Hōshi Ryokan, both in Japan.

Hot springs spa bath at Hōshi Ryokan, 3rd oldest hotel

Chapter 22

Weird Town Names

Some of the cities and towns in the United States have some of the strangest names.

Pennsylvania seems to hold the record for bizarre place names. There is Coupon, Pennsylvania, in Cambria County, with a population of 73. In addition, Mars is in Butler County, Pennsylvania with a population of 1,699.

There must be a sexy side to the state because Intercourse, Pennsylvania is in Lancaster County and has a population of 1,274. Also in Lancaster County is Blue Ball, with a population of 1,031 and Fertility, Pennsylvania. In the same vein is Lover, Pennsylvania, in Washington County, Beaver, Pennsylvania in Beaver County, and Climax in Armstrong County. There is also Virginville in Berks County, and has a population of 309.

Are you looking for Hell on Earth? Well, it used to be in California but it was demolished by the state to build a highway. However, Hell can still be found in Livingston County, Michigan. You can also find Hell in Norway, and Hell for Certain is in Leslie County, Kentucky.

Even though Hell is in Michigan, you can still find Paradise in Michigan. It is located in Chippewa County.

There is also a Paradise in Butte County, California, but unfortunately, as this is being written, almost the entire town was wiped out by the largest fire in California history, and possibly U.S. history.

Another Paradise is located in Cochise County, Arizona, but it is a ghost town.

There are actually a couple of other former towns in California called Paradise, in Butte County and Humboldt County.

But Paradise can be found all across the United States. Here are a list of states with Paradise locations.

Paradise, Illinois
Paradise, Indiana
Paradise, Kansas
Paradise, Kentucky
Paradise, Michigan
Paradise, Missouri
Paradise, Montana
Paradise, Nevada
Paradise, Ohio
Paradise, Oregon
Paradise, Pennsylvania
Paradise, Texas
Paradise, Utah
Paradise, Washington
Paradise, West Virginia
Paradise, Virgin Islands

If you want to know where Santa Claus lives, you might want to check out North Pole, Alaska, located near Fairbanks. It has a population of 2,232.

There is also a North Pole in Essex County, New York. It has a population of over 8,000.

Canada has some interesting place names, such as Stoner, British Columbia. It had that name long before Canada legalized marijuana. Interestingly, there is also a town of Stoner in Colorado, the first U.S. state to legalize recreational marijuana.

Ontario has some interesting towns such as Swastika, Crotch Lake, and Ball's Falls.

Quebec has a town called Saint-Louis-du-Ha! Ha! It is located near the Saint Lawrence River and has a population of 1,318.

Newfoundland and Labrador seems to have some extreme names for towns including Come By Chance, Dildo, and Blow Me Down.

The United Kingdom has some odd names also. Some of these names are pretty nasty, including the town of Nasty, which is located in the East Hertfordshire district. There is also Wetwang, Twatt, Brown Willy, Scratchy Bottom, Nob End, Crotch Crescent, Dicks Mount, Stranagalwilly, Crackpot, and Beer.

Finally, the country of Australia has some unusual place names. They include Mount Breast, Banana, Stonehenge, Boing Boing, Bong Bong, Burrumbuttock, Cock Wash, Wee Waa, and of course, The End of the World.

Chapter 23

The Woman Who Said No to Penthouse and Trump

You may not be familiar with her name, but Vera Coking is an important person in the area of real estate, and especially eminent domain. She stood up to two of the wealthiest people in the world.

She owned a boarding house in Atlantic City, New Jersey, which she and her husband had purchased for $20,000 back in 1961.

Bob Guccione, the founder and chairman of *Penthouse* magazine, acquired the property around hers in order to build the Penthouse Boardwalk Hotel and Casino. But Very Coking was the last holdout. She refused to sell.

Guccione offered her $1 million for her property but she still said no. So what did Guccione do? He began building the hotel and casino structure around her property.

Unfortunately for Guccione, construction stopped after only the steel framework for several stories were built, after running out of money in 1980.

In 1993, Donald Trump bought properties in the area to expend his casino but Coking refused to sell to him.

The city used eminent domain to take her property offering her $251,000. She fought the city with the help of the Institute of Justice, and eventually won.

In 2010, Coking moved out of her house and transferred it to her daughter, who listed it a year later for $5 million. After receiving no offers for two years, she dropped the price to $1 million.

Billionaire investor Carl Icahn eventually bought the property at auction in 2014 for $583,000. Four months later, he demolished it.

Coking House

Chapter 24

Trading a Paperclip for a House

You may had heard the story about the man who went through a series of bartering transactions, starting with one red paperclip, trading it, and ending up with a house.

This was done by a man in Canada named Kyle MacDonald. He has blogged about his story, One Red Paperclip, has written a book with the same name, and there is a movie in development with MGM

He started with the one red paperclip kept trading and trading until he ended up with a final barter for a house. The following is a list of items in each trading step.

    Red paperclip
    Fish-shaped pen
    Hand-sculpted doorknob
    Coleman camp stove
    Honda 1,000 watt generator
    Instant party package (included keg, beer of choice, and Budweiser sign
    Ski-Doo snowmobile
    Two person trip to Yahk, British Columbia
    Box truck
    Recording contract with Metalworks Studios
    Year's rent in Phoenix, Arizona
    One afternoon with Alice Cooper
    KISS motorized snow globe
    A role in the film, Donna on Demand
    A two-story house in Kipling, Saskatchewan

If you think he ended up with a shack, you would be wrong. The house has three bedrooms, two bathrooms, and a basement.

If you are ever in Kipling, Saskatchewan, the house can be found at 503 Main Street.

MacDonald covers all his trades in detail, both on his blog, oneredpaperclip.com, and his fascinating book.

Chapter 25

Islands

Largest Islands

You may think that Australia is an island, but because it is a continent, it is not considered to be one.

So the largest island is Greenland, measuring 822,700 square miles. It is a country within the Kingdom of Denmark. Even though it is the largest non-continental landmass, it is the least populated territory in the world, with a population of 56,480.

Nuuk, Capital of Greenland

The second, third fourth, and fifth largest islands are:

New Guinea
Borneo
Madagascar
Baffin Island

Smallest Island with a Commercial Building on It

The smallest island in the world that has a building on it is Bishop Rock, located in the Isles of Scilly, part of Cornwall, United Kingdom. The island has a 161 foot lighthouse on it, originally built in 1858.

The total size of the island is only 7,922 square feet. The lighthouse is now automated, so no one lives in it.

Bishop Rock Lighthouse - Richard Knights

* * *

Smallest Inhabited Island with a House

Just Room Enough Island, formerly known as Hub Island, has a great name that describes it perfectly, as there is just enough room for the house that is built on it.

This island in the Thousand Islands area near the Saint Lawrence River is the smallest inhabited island in the world. It is part of the state of New York, in Jefferson County.

The size of the island is approximately 3,300 square feet, less than half the size of Bishop Rock.

The property even has a very tiny beach.

Just Room Enough Island - User:Omegatron

Most Expensive Islands in the World

According to Private Islands Inc. the following are the most expensive islands, for those for which prices are disclosed.

Al Marjan Island is located in the United Arab Emirates. It is 115 acres in size, and is actually a collection of four man-made islands: Dream Island, Breeze Island, Treasure Island, and View Island. It is priced at a reasonable $462,000,000.

Dream Island – Al Marjan Island - ELPHNT

Rangyai Island is 110 acres and is located in Thailand. The price is $160,000,000.

In the United States, Pumpkin Key in Florida is 26 acres, and is priced at $95,000,000.

There is a large island in the Philippines called Apo Island. It is 2,147 acres and is available at $72,000,000.

The Spectabilis Island in The Exumas, in the Bahamas is for sale at $62,000,000. It is 460 acres.

Most Expensive Islands in the United States

According to Vladi Private Islands, in addition to the $95,000,000 Pumpkin Key previously mentioned, there are a couple other U.S. islands that sell for over ten million dollars.

Long Island, in Charleston County, South Carolina, is 147 acres of high ground, and is available at $19,900,000.

Petra Island, in Mahopac, New York, is 11 acres in size and has two houses on it plus a helipad. It is priced at $14,920,000.

Chapter 26

Miscellaneous Trivia

In the state of Florida, you are liable if your dog bites someone who is on your property unless you have a sign on your premises that includes the words "Bad Dog." Yes, those are the exact words the must be included on the sign according to Florida Statutes Title XLV. Torts § 767.04.

* * *

Doorknobs are a haven for germs. That's why they are made out of brass because of the anti-bacterial properties of the metal.

* * *

You are required to disclose if your house is haunted in the state of New York. This is according to the case of Stambovsky v. Ackley, 169 A.D.2d 254 (N.Y. App. Div. 1991), better known as the Ghostbusters ruling.

* * *

The oldest city in the United States is St. Augustine in Florida, founded in 1565.

* * *

The oldest continuously inhabited city in the world is Damascus, Syria, founded 11,000 years ago.

* * *

Vermont, Alaska, Hawaii, and Maine have laws against billboards.

* * *

Leona Helmsley, the "Queen of Mean" real estate investor, left $12 million to her Maltese dog, Trouble.

* * *

The Las Vegas Strip is not located in the city of Las Vegas. It is located in the towns of Paradise and Winchester.

* * *

Charles "Pretty Boy" Floyd, an American bank robber during the 1930s supposedly burned mortgages when he robbed banks.

* * *

The state that is the farthest east, west, and north is Alaska. It can be the farthest east and west because it crosses east of the Prime Meridian.

* * *

The word "mortgage" comes from the legal French term meaning "death pledge." It means that the mortgage agreement is dies, which is another way of saying completed, when it is either paid off or the property is foreclosed on.

* * *

A crematorium in Oslo, Norway tried to use heat from dead bodies to warm houses. However, the heat and power utility rejected it.

* * *

The term "housewarming party" comes from medieval times when friends would bring wood over to a new house to help warm the house by building a fire in the fireplace and would also help to ward off evil spirits.

* * *

Waldron Island, Washington has a law against having more than two toilets in your house.

* * *

In order to get a house sold in Ermelo, The Netherlands, the real estate broker built a roller coaster that would take you through the house.

* * *

In 2015, the United Church of Bacon tried to buy magician Penn Jillette's Las Vegas house.

* * *

It is illegal to raise pet rats in your home in Billings, Montana, unless you are feeding them to your reptiles or birds of prey.

* * *

In the state of California, home sellers are required to disclose to homebuyers if there was a murder or suicide in the house within the past three years, However, in Florida, such an event does not have to be disclosed.

* * *

It is illegal to fire cannon within 300 yards of a dwelling house in the United Kingdom. It is an offence under s 55 of the Metropolitan Police Act 1839.

* * *

In 1997, a real-life replica of the cartoon Simpsons house was constructed in Henderson, Nevada, and was offered as a grand prize in a contest. However, the winner of the contest decided to take the $75,000 alternative prize instead.

* * *

If you own a parcel of land in the United States, technically you own it all the way to the center of the earth.

"Cuius est solum, ejus est usque ad caelum et ad inferos":

"To whomever owns the land, shall own the earth to its center and up to the heavens."

Sources

Yahoo, Google, Zillow, and Wikipedia along with numerous other websites were used to confirm information that was used. The following includes some of the primary sources for most of the chapters.

Chapter 1 – 1 Square Inch of Land

"1 Square Inch of Land for Sale at $1,500," The Associated Press. Saturday, November 12, 2005; 10:21 PM
http://www.washingtonpost.com/wp-dyn/content/article/2005/11/12/AR2005111200636_pf.html
Retrieved November 11, 2018

Chapter 2 – 27.5 inch Long Triangle Parcel

Kim, Betsy (August 4–10, 2011). "Tiles Underfoot Recall Owner Who Put His Foot Down". The Villager. 81 (10). NYC Community Media.

Carlson, Jen (April 9, 2015). "The Story Behind Hess Triangle, Once The Littlest Piece Of Land In NYC". Gothamist.

"Hess Triangle". RoadsideAmerica.com.

Chapter 3 – Big Houses - Palaces

http://www.worldrecordacademy.com/biggest/largest_administrative_building_world_record_set_by_the_Palace_of_the_Romanian_Parliament_80185.htm

http://www.hotel-bucuresti.com/blog/2015/04/29/palatul-parlamentului-o-emblema-bucurestiului/

Douer, A.; Haupt, H. (1998). Wien, Heldenplatz: Mythen und Massen 1848-1998.

"A brief history - Hofburg | Wien | Österreich". hofburg-wien.at.

Bartholomew, James. The Richest Man in the World, Penguin Books Ltd; New Ed edition (February 22, 1990).

Chapter 4 – Big Houses - Castles

Castle of the Teutonic Order in Malbork https://whc.unesco.org/en/list/847.

"10 Largest Castles in the World (with Photos & Map) - Touropia". touropia.com.

Chapter 5 – Biggest Mansion in the World

"A peek into Shraddha Sharma US $1 bn Mumbai home". Rediff.com.

Mumbai Billionaire's Home Boasts 34 Floors, Ocean and Slum Views by Mark Magnier, Los Angeles Times, 24 October 2010

"The World's Most Expensive, Forbes Magazine". Forbes. https://www.forbes.com/sites/erincarlyle/2014/05/13/the-most-expensive-billionaire-homes-in-the-world/#c038a806afad

Headlines Today Bureau. "Mukesh Ambani all set to move into world's costliest house: India : India Today". Indiatoday.intoday.in.

Spillett, Richard (4 November 2014). "World's most expensive homes". Daily Mail. dailymail.co.uk.

Woolsey, Matt (30 April 2008). "Inside The World's First Billion-Dollar Home". Forbes. Forbes.com.

"Mittal's address more expensive than Ambani's – Money – DNA". Dnaindia.com.

Chapter 6 – Biggest Mansion in the US

https://www.biltmore.com/visit/biltmore-house-gardens/estate-history

Chapter 7 – Smallest Town Sold

"Buy Buford, America's Smallest Town, For a Paltry $100K" Curbed.com
https://www.curbed.com/2012/4/4/10382576/buy-buford-americas-smallest-town-for-a-paltry-100k

Wyomingnews.com
https://www.wyomingnews.com/news/phindeli-town-buford-open-for-business/article_e7f79e6e-6dfb-5c1c-910f-2bf888350af8.html#.VICflzHF91Y

Rosenfeld, Everett (July 20, 2011). "Meet the Only Resident of America's Smallest Town". TIME.

Chapter 8 – Red Front Door

https://patch.com/california/shermanoaks/what-does-a-red-front-door-mean

https://www.acepaintsfurniture.com/the-meaning-of-a-red-front-door/

http://www.santaclaritamagazine.com/2017/02/red-door-mean-history-origin-meaning-red-front-door/

Chapter 9 – Lighthouses

Placemakers: Emperors, Kings, Entrepreneurs: A Brief History of Real Estate Development (Figure 1 Publishing Inc., 2017)

http://theweeklybookscan.blogs.realtor.org/2017/06/07/a-history-of-the-world-via-real-estate/

Clayton, Peter A. (2013). "Chapter 7: The Pharos at Alexandria". In Peter A. Clayton; Martin J. Price. The Seven Wonders of the Ancient World. London: Routledge.

"A Unique Vacation Home Away from All Civilization." November 09, 2007
http://billionaireslife.blogspot.com/2007/11/unique-vacation-home-away-from-all.html

"New York Island May Be Available for Sale." May 20, 2010
http://billionaireslife.blogspot.com/2010/05/new-york-island-may-be-available-for.html

Chapter 10 – Winchester Mystery House

"Winchester Mystery House". Frommer's.

Hawes, Jason; Wilson, Grant; Friedman, Michael Jan (2007). "The Winchester Mystery July 2005". Ghost Hunting: True Stories of Unexplained Phenomena from The Atlantic Paranormal Society. New York: Pocket Books.

McAndrew, Frank (29 Jan 2018). "The Winchester Myster House and Other Haunged Places: Why do some places feel as if they were intentionally designed to creep us out?". Psychology Today.

https://www.neighborhoods.com/blog/take-a-tour-of-san-joses-winchester-mystery-house/about/

San Jose Mercury News: "One Less Mystery: Two Prominent Families Own San Jose's Mystery House." April 26, 1997

"New room found at San Jose's Winchester Mystery House". abc7news.com. October 10, 2016.

https://winchestermysteryhouse.com/sarahs-story/

https://winchestermysteryhouse.com/timeline/

http://mentalfloss.com/article/527411/14-haunting-facts-about-winchester-mystery-house

Chapter 11 – Most Expensive US House

https://www.thesun.co.uk/money/5729336/worlds-most-expensive-home-the-one/

https://la.curbed.com/2018/10/25/18021054/most-expensive-house-for-sale-bel-air

https://www.propertyshark.com/Real-Estate-Reports/2018/10/17/here-is-the-most-expensive-home-for-sale-in-each-state-the-district-of-columbia/

Jade Mills Estates
https://www.jademillsestates.com/property/chartwell-estate

Chapter 12 – Quotes

https://inboundrem.com/top-50-real-estate-quotes-time/

https://www.brainyquote.com/topics/real_estate

Chapter 13 – Monopoly

Pilon, Mary (February 13, 2015). "Monopoly's Inventor: The Progressive Who Didn't Pass 'Go'". The New York Times.

Orbanes, Philip E. (2006). Monopoly: The World's Most Famous Game & How it Got that Way. Da Capo Press.

Brian McMahon (November 29, 2007). "How board game helped free POWs".

Ki Mae Heussner (September 18, 2009). "Get Out of Jail Free: Monopoly's Hidden Maps". ABC News.

Seay, Elizabeth (September 28, 1998). "Get on Board". Wall Street Journal.

Horton, J. Matthew. "1999–2008". Monopoly History. worldofmonopoly.com

Stromberg, Joseph. "The Jeweled Art of Sidney Mobell". Smithsonian.

Chapter 14 – Buffett

https://www.businessinsider.com/warren-buffett-modest-home-bought-31500-looks-2017-6

https://www.ocregister.com/2018/10/12/warren-buffett-sells-laguna-beach-home-for-7-47-million/

https://www.cnbc.com/2017/05/27/see-inside-warren-buffetts-laguna-beach-house-on-sale-for-11-million.html

https://www.fool.com/investing/2018/08/24/why-is-this-the-only-reit-in-warren-buffetts-portf.aspx

https://www.bloomberg.com/news/articles/2018-03-29/buffett-s-home-brokerage-booms-with-the-no-1-ranking-in-sight

https://www.cnbc.com/2017/03/06/heres-why-warren-buffett-thinks-you-should-buy-a-home.html

Chapter 15 – 3D Printed Houses

Benedict. "AMT-SPECAVIA builds Europe's first habitable 3D printed building". 3ders.org.

3DPrinthuset (Denmark) - https://3dprinthuset.dk/europes-first-3d-printed-building/

Chapter 16 – Tiniest house

https://smallesthouseintheworld.com

"Too Tiny? Boston Artist Builds 'Smallest House in the World'" By Claudine Zap | Apr 29, 2016
https://www.realtor.com/news/unique-homes/smallest-house-in-the-world/

Chapter 17 – Narrowest house

"Dom Kereta / Keret House". Centrala

"Check Out The Skinniest House In The World". Co.DESIGN.
https://www.fastcompany.com/1664572/check-out-the-skinniest-house-in-the-world

"Perfect for a size-zero model: World's skinniest house is just five feet across ... and barely has enough room for a kitchen". Daily Mail Online. London. 19 October 2012.

Chapter 18 – White House

Frary, Ihna Thayer (1969). They Built the Capitol. Ayer Publishing. p. 27. ISBN 978-0-8369-5089-2.

Seale, William (1992). The White House, The History of an American Idea. The American Institute of Architects Press. pp. 35. 1. ISBN 978-1-55835-049-6.

"White House Facts". The White House.

"Technology: 1980s". White House Historical Association.

Shenkman, Richard and Reiger, Kurt. *One-Night Stands with American History*. 2003.

Chapter 19 – Ice Houses

Business brisk at Quebec's 'ice hotel', CBC, January 2, 2001

Ice Hotel Is Tourist Hotspot, CBS News, Brian Dakss, January 6, 2006

"An ice place to visit... But you may not want to stay more than a few days," Los Angeles Times, Feb 9, 2003

Staying Cool: Sweden's ICEHOTEL Is One of the Country's Seven Wonders
https://www.good.is/articles/staying-cool-sweden-s-icehotel-is-one-of-the-country-s-seven-wonders

Chapter 20 – First Motel

Jackson, Kristin (April 25, 1993). "The World's First Motel Rests Upon Its Memories". The Seattle Times.

"Photos from the Vault: Motel Inn in San Luis Obispo, the world's first 'mo-tel'". San Luis Obispo Tribune. December 4, 2014.

Zorn, Eric (August 15, 2006). "World's first motel a site worth saving". Chicago Tribune.

Chapter 21 – First Hotel

https://www.keiunkan.co.jp

https://www.keiunkan.co.jp/en/

http://www.guinnessworldrecords.com/world-records/oldest-hotel

Morris, Chris. The World's Oldest Hotel Has Been a Family Business for 1,300 Years Fortune. 16 January 2016

Chapter 23 – The Woman Who Said No

Matt A.V. Chaban (July 21, 2014). "A Homeowner's Refusal to Cash Out in a Gambling Town Proves Costly". The New York Times.

"Public Power, Private Gain: The Abuse of Eminent Domain". Institute for Justice.

"IN BRIEF; Follow-Ups: Judge Rejects Property Seizure". The New York Times, July 26, 1998.

Nelson, I. Rose (1998). "Court Condemns Casino Condemnations". The Gambling and the Law.

Herszenhorn, David M. (July 21, 1998). "Widowed Homeowner Foils Trump in Atlantic City", The New York Times.

Wittkowski, Donald (August 28, 2011). "Empty Atlantic City boarding home near casinos selling for $5 million". The Press of Atlantic City.

Cohen, Lauren (September 24, 2013). "Asking price drops on house Vera Coking refused to sell to Trump". The Press of Atlantic City.

Wittkowski, Donald (16 February 2016). "Coveted by developers, Atlantic City rooming house finally falls to wreckers". The Press of Atlantic City.

NBC10 Philadelphia (November 20, 2014). "Atlantic City House of Woman Who Heldout Against Donald Trump Comes Down". NBC10 (Philadelphia).

"Thousands out of work in Atlantic City as big casinos shut doors". Atlantic City News. 1 September 2014.

Chapter 24 – Red Paperclip

MacDonald, Kyle. *One Red Paperclip: How To Trade a Red Paperclip For a House.* 2015.

One Red Paperclip.
http://oneredpaperclip.blogspot.com

https://www.cbc.ca/news/canada/from-paper-clip-to-house-in-14-trades-1.573973

http://news.bbc.co.uk/2/hi/technology/5167388.stm

Chapter 25 – Islands

"The Funny Story Behind the World's Smallest Island." Condé Nast Traveler.
https://www.cntraveler.com/stories/2014-03-24/bishop-rock-isles-scilly-england

"World's 7 most dangerous and remote islands". CNN.com.

"Bishop Rock: The Smallest Island in the World". amusingplanet.com.

"World's Smallest Inhabited Island Is About the Size of a Tennis Court"
https://www.msn.com/en-us/travel/news/worlds-smallest-inhabited-island-is-about-the-size-of-a-tennis-court/ar-BBGB7Ao

https://www.privateislandsonline.com/search?availability=sale

https://www.vladi-private-islands.de/en/islands-for-sale/usa/

Chapter 26 – Miscellaneous

http://sciencenetlinks.com/science-news/science-updates/antibacterial-doorknobs/

https://property1.wordpress.com/2015/10/21/do-brass-doorknobs-disinfect-themselves/

https://wonderopolis.org/wonder/where-is-the-oldest-city-in-the-united-states

https://www.mnn.com/lifestyle/eco-tourism/stories/12-oldest-continuously-inhabited-cities

https://money.cnn.com/galleries/2007/fortune/0712/gallery.101_dumbest.fortune/3.html

https://www.thelocal.no/20150325/oslo-crematorium

https://www.redfin.com/blog/2016/12/6-weird-real-estate-laws-that-are-actually-on-the-books.html

https://www.codepublishing.com/WA/SanJuanCounty/html/SanJuanCounty16/SanJuanCounty1636.html

https://www.thrillist.com/entertainment/nation/weird-state-laws
https://codes.findlaw.com/fl/title-xlv-torts/fl-st-sect-767-04.html

https://www.today.com/home/roller-coaster-house-netherlands-aims-entice-prospective-buyers-1D80340037

https://webcache.googleusercontent.com/search?q=cache:zTCtSO_dMgAJ:https://www.realtor.com/news/trends/wackiest-real-estate-stories-of-2015/+&cd=11&hl=en&ct=clnk&gl=us&client=safari

https://library.municode.com/mt/billings/codes/code_of_ordinances?nodeId=CICO_CH4AN_ART4-300CAKESAAN_S4-304RARA

http://www.lawcom.gov.uk/app/uploads/2015/03/Legal_Oddities.pdf

https://maps.roadtrippers.com/stories/visit-the-real-life-full-size-simpsons-house

http://www.duhaime.org/LegalResources/RealEstateTenancy/LawArticle-66/Air-Water-and-Subsurface-Rights.aspx

Picture Credits

Chapter 2 – Smallest Parcel in NYC

Wikimedia Commons - Bogframe
Creative Commons Attribution-Share Alike 3.0

Chapter 3 – Big Houses - Palaces

hpgruesen - https://pixabay.com/ro/bucure%C8%99ti-parlamentul-palatul-1280226/
CC0 1.0 Universal (CC0 1.0) Public Domain Dedication

Chapter 4 – Biggest Castle

Vorburg with rampart added under Hochmeister Heinrich von Plauen, 15th century – Mewes – public domain

Chapter 5 – Biggest Mansion in the World

©A.Savin, Wikimedia Commons
Free Art License 1.3
https://commons.wikimedia.org/wiki/File:Mumbai_03-2016_19_Antilia_Tower.jpg

Chapter 6 – Biggest US Mansion

Biltmore Estate - 24dupontchevy -via Wikipedia
Attribution-ShareAlike 4.0 International (CC BY-SA 4.0)

https://en.wikipedia.org/wiki/Biltmore_Estate#/media/File:Biltmore_Estate,_Asheville,_North_Carolina.jpg

Chapter 7 – Smallest Town Sold

Flickr - Mark Brennan - Attribution-ShareAlike 2.0 Generic (CC BY-SA 2.0)

Chapter 9 - Lighthouses

A drawing of the Pharos of Alexandria by German archaeologist Prof. H. Thiersch (1909).

Plum Island Animal Disease Center (aerial view), photo from http://www.ars.usda.gov/plum/

Chapter 10 – Winchester Mystery House

http://www.cr.nps.gov/nr/travel/santaclara/win.htm

Chapter 11 – Most Expensive House for Sale

Beverly Hillbillies Mansion – Photo by Alan Light. Attribution 2.0 Generic (CC BY 2.0)

Chapter 13 - Monopoly

U.S. Patent and Trademark Office

Chapter 14 – Warren Buffett

The White House from Washington, DC - P071811PS-0254 Official White House Photo by Pete Souza – Public Domain

Chapter 15 – 3D Printed Houses

AMT-SPETSAVIA Group (Russia) - www.specavia.pro
The first living building in Europe printed with a 3D construction printer. Yaroslavl (Russia)
Creative Commons Attribution-Share Alike 4.0 International license

3DPrinthuset (Denmark) - https://3dprinthuset.dk/europes-first-3d-printed-building/

Chapter 17 – Narrowest House

Panek - Own work
Keret House in Warsaw.
Attribution-ShareAlike 3.0 Unported (CC BY-SA 3.0)

Chapter 18 – White House

http://www.whitehouse.gov/news/releases/2001/12/images/20011202-1.html
Public Domain

Chapter 20 – First Motel

Tichnor Brothers, Publisher - Boston Public Library Tichnor Brothers collection #80459 – Public Domain

Chapter 21 – First Hotel

Akiyoshi's Room - Akiyoshi's Room
Hōshi Onsen in Minakami, Gunma, Japan.
Public Domain

Chapter 23 – The Woman Who Said No

Coking house at 127 S Columbia Pl, between the steel framework of the planned Penthouse Casino; photographed by Jack Boucher for Historic American Buildings Survey, c.1991 Public Domain

Chapter 25 – Islands

Nuuk - Oliver Schauf - Own work – Public Domain

Bishop Rock Lighthouse - Richard Knights - Attribution-ShareAlike 2.0 Generic (CC BY-SA 2.0)

Just Room Enough Island
User:Omegatron - Taken by User:Omegatron using a Canon Powershot SD110 - Own work
Attribution-ShareAlike 3.0 Unported (CC BY-SA 3.0)

Dream Island – Al Marjan Island - ELPHNT
Attribution-ShareAlike 4.0 International (CC BY-SA 4.0)

Cover

Photo by Fidelia Zheng on Unsplash

Photo by Kyle Mills on Unsplash

Photo by Micaela Parente via Unsplash

Photo by Michael D Beckwith on Unsplash

ABOUT THE AUTHOR

Fred Fuld III is a financial historian. He was a former executive in the financial services industry who started out working as a stockbroker, and later as a market maker on the options floor of the Pacific Stock Exchange. He then became vice president of a San Francisco based investment management firm. He also worked as an adjunct professor for the College of Business of a California State University.

He has owned all types of real estate, including single family residential, multi-family residential, condominium, commercial, land, tax lien, and gold mining claims.

He is the publisher of WallStreetNewsNetwork.com and Stockerblog.com, and has written numerous articles for various publications, including Friends of Financial History Magazine, the Bond and Share Society Journal, and Scripophily Magazine. Television appearances include CNBC, Fox Business News, and Globo TV.

He has given speeches at the Museum of American Finance in New York City, The Money Show in both San Francisco and Las Vegas, California State University East Bay, and numerous other venues.

fredfuld.com

www.ingramcontent.com/pod-product-compliance
Lightning Source LLC
Chambersburg PA
CBHW071417220526
45469CB00004B/1307